SUPERCOPTERS

PAUL HARRISON

ARCTURUS

First published in 2015 by Arcturus Publishing

Distributed by Black Rabbit Books.

P. O. Box 3263
Mankato
Minnesota MN 56002

Printed in China

Cataloging-in-Publication Data is available from the Library of Congress
ISBN: 978-1-78404-077-2

Text: Paul Harrison
Editor: Joe Harris
Assistant editor: Frances Evans
Picture research: Mirco De Cet
Design: sprout.uk.com
Cover design: sprout.uk.com

Picture credits
AgustaWestland: cover, 20b, 20–21c, 21t. Boeing: 28–29c. Corbis: 8c (Wojtek Lembryk/epa), 9c (ANATOLY MALTSEV/epa), 12bl (David Billinge/Demotix), 12–13c (Jim Orr / Demotix/Demotix), 13tr (George Hall), 14c (Kent Porter/ZUMA Pres), 15c (Randy Pench/ZUMA Press). Eurocopter: 3, 4c, 5t, 18c, 19t, 19b. Juergen Lehle (albspotter.eu): 16–17. Regular Daddy: 22–23c. Shutterstock: 26c and 27b (Anatoliy Lukich). U.S. Air Force photo: 6t and 7c (Senior airman Julianne Showalter), 25t (Staff Sgt. Thomas Trower), 25b (Senior Airman Steven R. Doty). U.S. Army photo: 24c. USDOD: 23t. US Marine Corp: 30c. US National Archives: 31c.

SL004075US

Supplier 29, Date 0514, Print run 3420

CONTENTS

EUROCOPTER X3 **4**

BELL BOEING V-22 OSPREY **6**

MIL MI-26 HALO **8**

MOSQUITO AIR **10**

AGUSTAWESTLAND SEA KING **12**

BELL HUEY UH-1H SUPER HUEY **14**

MD902 EXPLORER **16**

EUROCOPTER EC 135 **18**

AGUSTAWESTLAND AW101 VVIP **20**

ERIKSON S-64 AIR-CRANE **22**

BOEING CH-47 CHINOOK **24**

MBB BO-105 **26**

BOEING SIKORSKY RAH-66 COMANCHE **28**

KAMAN K-MAX UAS **30**

GLOSSARY/FURTHER READING/INDEX **32**

EUROCOPTER X3

Supercopters are the most incredible vertical takeoff vehicles in the world. The Eurocopter X3 may look a little weird—that's because it has more engines and more rotors than most helicopters. This means more power and of course more power equals more speed!

The engines are made by Rolls–Royce, which is a famous luxury car manufacturer.

The X3 is designed as a rapid response helicopter—handy for rescues or for military use.

The X3 is a prototype, which is an experimental vehicle used to test new technology and design.

Short wings keep the forward rotors away from the main body of the helicopter.

X3 broke the unofficial helicopter speed record by hitting 255 knots—which is an amazing 293 mph (472 km/h).

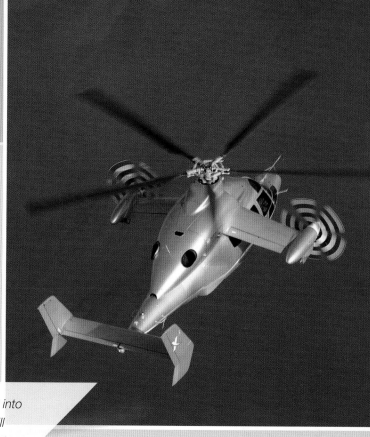

It's not just the number of rotors that makes the X3 so fast—it's the way they are arranged. There is large rotor on top. This allows the helicopter to go straight up and down—or vertical takeoff and landing as it is called. Two rotors at the side work like an aeroplane's propellers, pulling the helicopter through the air.

There are no plans to put the X3 into production. Instead, Eurocopter will design a new helicopter based on what it has discovered from the X3.

The two sets of forward facing rotors keep the helicopter stable. They also help it move forward.

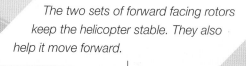

SUPER STATS

EUROCOPTER X3
TOP SPEED: 293 mph (472 km/h)
POWERED BY: 2 x Rolls–Royce engines
ENGINE POWER: 2,270 horsepower
CREW: 2
PASSENGERS: 8
MAXIMUM ALTITUDE: 12,500 feet
(3,810 m)
MADE IN: France

BELL BOEING V-22 OSPREY

Is it a helicopter or a plane? Actually, it's a supercopter called the V-22 Osprey. The Osprey has a unique way of turning its rotor blades around to get the best of both worlds. It has the vertical lift of a helicopter, plus the straight-line speed and range of a propeller plane. This makes it a really versatile machine that is both useful and quick.

The swiveling engines are known as tiltrotors.

There's space for 9.9 tons (9 tonnes) of cargo inside.

The Osprey is designed to carry either passengers or cargo.

Swiveling rotors aren't the only clever bits of technology on the Osprey. This supercopter has been designed so that it can still fly even if one of its engines fails. Helicopters need two sets of rotors to fly. But the Osprey's one good engine can power both sets of rotors to keep the supercopter in the air.

Up to 7.5 tons (6.8 tonnes) of cargo can be carried under the Osprey.

The super-flexible Osprey has proved to be popular with the military.

The wings and rotors can be folded away to make storing the Osprey easier.

SUPER STATS

BELL BOEING V-22 OSPREY
TOP SPEED: 287mph (463 km/h)
POWERED BY: 2 x Rolls–Royce engines
ENGINE POWER: 6,150 horsepower
CREW: Up to 3
PASSENGERS: 24
MAXIMUM ALTITUDE: 25,000 feet (7,620 m)
MADE IN: USA

MIL MI-26 HALO

Supercopters don't get any bigger than the enormous MIL Mi-26 Halo. It's the largest helicopter flying in the skies today. The Mi-26 is a helicopter that was built to carry heavy loads. Thanks to its gigantic size, there are no other helicopters that can do or carry what this supercopter can!

The huge cargo hold measures 39 feet (12 m) long and 10.5 feet (3.2 m) wide.

The Mi-26's massive rotor is 105 feet (32 m) in diameter.

The Mi-26 is useful as a rescue vehicle. It has space for up to sixty stretchers.

The tail skid at the back protects the end of the tail from getting bashed on the ground during takeoff or landing.

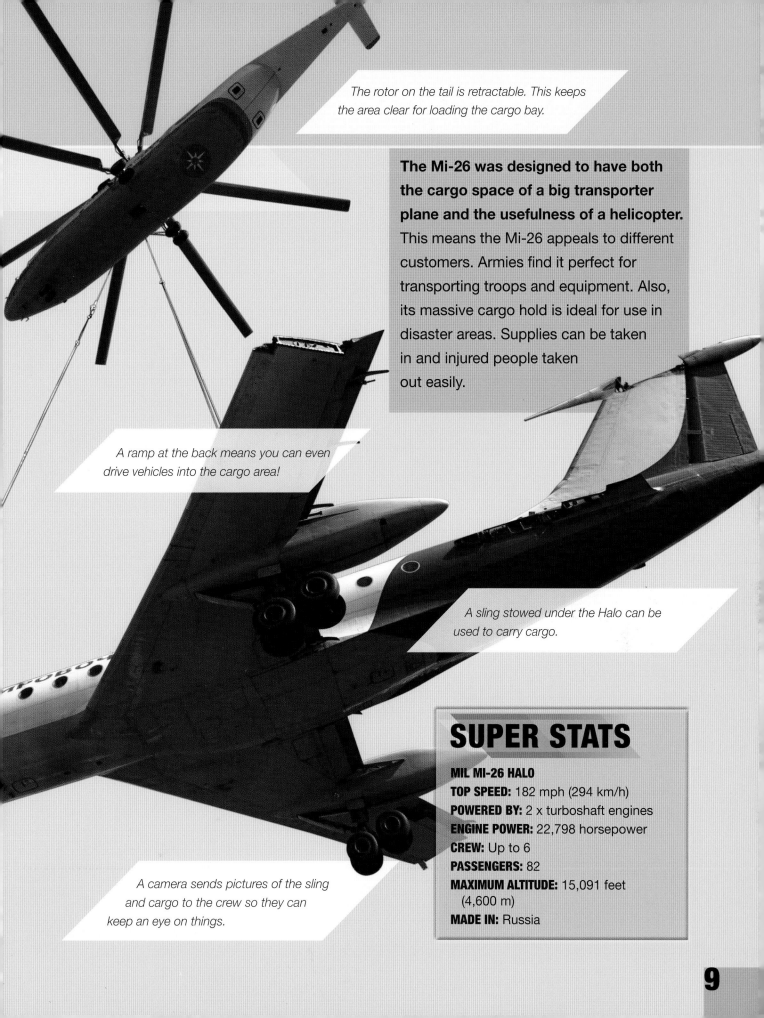

The rotor on the tail is retractable. This keeps the area clear for loading the cargo bay.

The Mi-26 was designed to have both the cargo space of a big transporter plane and the usefulness of a helicopter. This means the Mi-26 appeals to different customers. Armies find it perfect for transporting troops and equipment. Also, its massive cargo hold is ideal for use in disaster areas. Supplies can be taken in and injured people taken out easily.

A ramp at the back means you can even drive vehicles into the cargo area!

A sling stowed under the Halo can be used to carry cargo.

A camera sends pictures of the sling and cargo to the crew so they can keep an eye on things.

SUPER STATS

MIL MI-26 HALO
TOP SPEED: 182 mph (294 km/h)
POWERED BY: 2 x turboshaft engines
ENGINE POWER: 22,798 horsepower
CREW: Up to 6
PASSENGERS: 82
MAXIMUM ALTITUDE: 15,091 feet (4,600 m)
MADE IN: Russia

MOSQUITO AIR

If you think that all helicopters are big, complicated machines, then you've never seen the Mosquito Air! This ultralight vehicle is one of the smallest helicopters in the world. It has so few parts, you'll feel as if you're flying like a bird rather than scooting around in a machine.

The Mosquito Air is made from aluminum tubing and carbon fiber. Both materials are strong but very light.

In some countries, you don't even need a special licence to fly the Air. That's because it's so small and carries so little fuel.

There are other Mosquito helicopters that are similar to the Air. However, these come with a body, windshield, and even floats for landing on water!

Three legs keep the Mosquito Air off the ground.

Although the Air's engine is small, the helicopter is so light that the engine has enough power to get you into the air.

If there were no small rotor at the back of the tail, the helicopter would just spin around and around.

The Mosquito Air was originally designed as a build-it-yourself kit for people to make at home. No specialist knowledge or tools are needed (except some welding equipment). It takes around 200 hours to build the Air. However, for those people without the basic skills—or a welding torch—the company sells ready-made Airs so everyone can enjoy one!

The small metal feet at the ends of the legs are called skid plates.

SUPER STATS

MOSQUITO AIR
TOP SPEED: 69.8 mph (112.6 km/h)
POWERED BY: 1 x two-cylinder engine
ENGINE POWER: 60 horsepower
CREW: 1
PASSENGERS: 0
MAXIMUM ALTITUDE: Around 8,000 feet (2,438 m)
MADE IN: New Zealand

MEAN MACHINES

AGUSTAWESTLAND
SEA KING

If you were in trouble at sea or lost on the moors, there's one supercopter you'd want to rescue you—the AgustaWestland Sea King. The Sea King provides 24 hour search and rescue support around Britain. It is equipped with all the technology needed to find and rescue anyone who is in difficulty. In short, the Sea King is a supercopter hero!

A search and rescue Sea King has a crew of four. There are two pilots, plus one person operating the radar and another operating the winch.

There is enough space inside to carry 22 people or nine on stretchers.

ROYAL NAVY
RESCU
ZA130

The Sea King has an infrared camera that detects body heat.

The infrared camera is useful for finding people when weather conditions make it hard to see.

Sea Kings have been in operation since the 1960s. However, these supercopters are no longer made. Despite this, air forces around the world are still using this model because it's so useful and reliable. Differently equipped Sea Kings are also used to hunt submarines. Others act as mobile early warning systems—that's one super-versatile supercopter!

Pilots wear night-vision goggles to help them fly in the dark.

The Sea King is equipped with a winch for lifting people aboard.

SUPER STATS

AGUSTAWESTLAND SEA KING
TOP SPEED: 144 mph (232 km/h)
POWERED BY: 2 x Rolls–Royce engines
ENGINE POWER: 2,778 horsepower
CREW: 4
PASSENGERS: 22
MAXIMUM ALTITUDE: 10,000 feet (3,048 m)
MADE IN: UK/Italy

BELL HUEY
UH-1H SUPER HUEY

The UH-1H Super Huey might well be the fastest fire engine around. This firefighting supercopter is specially set up to tackle forest fires. These fires are often out of reach to normal fire trucks. Also, they're usually too far away to get to quickly. That's when you need a supercopter like the Super Huey to bring the flames under control and keep people safe.

The Super Huey can carry up to 3,000 lbs (1,360 kg) of weight on the outside.

A winch can be lowered to rescue people on the ground or to attach a stretcher.

The Super Huey has a range of around 250 miles (400 km). That means it can travel 125 miles (200 km) and return home on just one tank of fuel.

The Super Huey can carry a nine-person fire crew. They can then be dropped at the scene of a blaze .

The Super Huey can carry a 340-gallon (1,226 l) bucket of water or firefighting foam. This is hung from below the helicopter and tipped onto the flames.

Although it's brilliant at firefighting, the Super Huey was not designed to tackle forest fires. During the Vietnam War (1959-1975) it was used by the military for a variety of purposes. The Super Huey proved to be such a supercopter that, after the war, lots of surplus helicopters were bought. These were converted to do jobs such as firefighting.

A large tank inside the helicopter can hold up to 368 gallons (1,324 l) of water or foam.

When it isn't fighting fires, the Super Huey can be used for search and rescue missions.

SUPER STATS

BELL HUEY UH-1H SUPER HUEY
TOP SPEED: 138 mph (222 km/h)
POWERED BY: 1 turboshaft engine
ENGINE POWER: 1,800 horsepower
CREW: 1 pilot + 2 fire captains + 8 firefighters
PASSENGERS: 0
MAXIMUM ALTITUDE: Around 19,390 feet (5,900 m)
MADE IN: Dubai

MD902 EXPLORER

The MD902 Explorer is a real crime-fighting supercopter! This versatile helicopter is one of the police's most useful vehicles. It's equipped with all sorts of gadgets specially designed to keep track of criminals down below. The long arm of the law stretches right down from the sky when the Explorer's on duty!

The Explorer doesn't have a tail rotor. Instead, it uses a fan on its tail and air is blown down by the main rotors to keep the helicopter stable. Not having a tail rotor is safer as it means no one can be hit by it.

At night, infrared cameras are used to track criminals. These cameras show body heat rather than a visual image.

Many helicopters suffer from vibration as they hover. Not the MD902. This makes it an ideal supercopter as it can keep a steady position over the action.

A bright searchlight attached to the Explorer is useful for highlighting areas at night.

Chasing criminals can be tricky, but not with this supercopter. Being a helicopter, the Explorer doesn't have to stick to roads. It can hover over the action, keeping an eye on what's going on down below. The crew inside the Explorer is usually made up of a pilot of course, a police officer, and a paramedic. That means the Explorer can help out in medical emergencies too.

The Explorer keeps in radio communication with police on the ground. That way it can direct them to where they are needed.

The body of the Explorer contains a thin aluminum mesh, which provides protection against lightning strikes.

D-HBWC

Some MD Explorers are also used as air ambulances. The inside can be altered to fit a stretcher too.

SUPER STATS

MD902 EXPLORER
TOP SPEED: 161 mph (259 km/h)
POWERED BY: 2 x Pratt and
   Whitney engines
ENGINE POWER: 1,100 horsepower
CREW: 2
PASSENGERS: 6
MAXIMUM ALTITUDE: 20,000 feet
   (6,096 m)
MADE IN: USA

MEAN MACHINES

EUROCOPTER EC 135

If you're really rich, then you will need a supercopter to fly you around. It's a great way of getting to the places that private jets can't—like the tops of tall office buildings. One of the best that you can get is the Eurocopter EC 135. It's light, relatively cheap to run, spacious, and it can be adapted to suit your needs.

The rotor blades sit high above the ground, which stops people being hit by the blades. For added safety, the rear rotors sit inside a covering called a shroud.

Two doors at the back open to reveal a space for luggage.

For a helicopter, the EC 135 is very quiet. This is handy when flying over cities as you don't disturb people.

The EC 135 is also used by some police forces.

EC 135 can carry a satellite telephone on board for making important business calls on the move.

The huge windows give passengers and the pilot an excellent view.

You can arrange the inside of the EC 135 any way that you like. That means it can be used by emergency services around the world as it can fit stretchers inside. However, it really works well as a private aircraft, ferrying business workers from one meeting to another. And the better paid the workers, the more luxurious the EC 135 can be!

D-HVBX

F-HERO

The number of passenger seats can be adjusted depending on the customer. The EC 135 can seat up to seven people comfortably.

SUPER STATS

EUROCOPTER EC 135
TOP SPEED: 161 mph (259 km/h)
POWERED BY: 2 x Pratt and Whitney engines
ENGINE POWER: 816 horsepower
CREW: Up to 2
PASSENGERS: Up to 7
MAXIMUM ALTITUDE: 10,000 feet (3,048 m)
MADE IN: Germany

AGUSTAWESTLAND AW101 VVIP

The AW101 VVIP is a special helicopter for very special people. How special? The clue is in the name—VVIP stands for Very, Very Important Person. Leaders of countries and even royalty choose the AW 101 VVIP as their go-to helicopter. The reason is that it's one of the most luxurious supercopters in the sky.

A weather radar system is installed inside the nose of the AW101. That way the crew knows if bad weather is coming before they can see it.

There are doors to the side and rear.

The cabin is 6 feet (1.83 m) high inside. That might not sound a lot but it's bigger than most private jets.

The AW101 is armor-plated for protection-- and the seats can be armor-plated too!

As you might expect with a luxury supercopter, the interior of the AW101 is made to the customer's needs. The type and number of seats inside and how they are laid out are all decisions for the buyer. If you want wardrobes and a shower you can have them—but all this comes at a price. Costs vary according to what is included, but you will need around $19 million if you want to buy one of these luxury supercopters.

Windows can be dimmed electronically, which is handy for both privacy and catching a nap.

External cameras allow passengers and crew to keep an eye on things outside.

The tail is high enough for a limousine to pull right up to the rear doors.

SUPER STATS

AGUSTAWESTLAND AW101 VVIP
TOP SPEED: 172 mph (278 km/h)
POWERED BY: 3 x engines
ENGINE POWER: 7,500 horsepower
CREW: 2
PASSENGERS: Up to 30
MAXIMUM ALTITUDE: 15,000 feet (4,572 m)
MADE IN: UK/Italy

MEAN MACHINES

ERIKSON S-64 AIR-CRANE

The S-64's unique looks make it a "one of a kind" type of helicopter. It might look as if it has a big chunk missing out of it but it's been designed that way. The S64 is called an Air-Crane and sometimes a skycrane. Part of its body can be swapped depending on what it is being used for. This supercopter has proved to be useful for both military and civilian purposes.

Since 1992, Air-Cranes have been given names. One of the most famous is called Elvis and works as a firefighting helicopter in Australia.

Air-Cranes have been useful in disaster situations as well as for construction.

The crane can lift can lift about 10 tons (9.1 tonnes)—it's strong enough to carry a helicopter!

The S-64 isn't very fast, but this supercopter was designed for its lifting ability rather than for its speed!

ERICKSON AIR-CRANE

Air-Cranes were originally made by famous helicopter manufacturer Sikorsky. Now they are made by Erickson.

Apart from carrying heavy objects to places that other cranes can't reach, the S-64 is also a versatile supercopter. When it isn't being used as a crane, the helicopter can have attachments fitted underneath it. A pod to carry passengers can be added, or a water tank that turns it into a firefighting machine.

At the back of the cockpit, a rear-facing seat is used by one of the crew to operate the grappling hook.

A strong grapple hangs from the middle of the S-64 for carrying heavy objects.

SUPER STATS

ERIKSON S-64 AIR-CRANE
TOP SPEED: 132 mph (213 km/h)
POWERED BY: 2 x Prat and Whitney engines
ENGINE POWER: 9,000 horsepower
CREW: 3
PASSENGERS: 2
MAXIMUM ALTITUDE: 31,480 feet (9,595 m)
MADE IN: Dubai

BOEING CH-47 CHINOOK

With its twin rotor blades, the Chinook is probably the most easily recognizable helicopter in the world. For more than fifty years, this supercopter has been used both by the military and by civilian companies. That's because this amazing helicopter has proved itself to be both super-reliable and very versatile.

There are three cargo hooks below the Chinook for attaching external cargo.

The Chinook is a record-breaker: no other Boeing helicopter has been in continuous production for so long.

The two sets of propellers are called "tandem rotors."

The tandem rotor system means the Chinook can fly in conditions that may be too extreme for other helicopters.

The Chinook can carry cargo weighing over 9.4 tons (8.5 tonnes).

The Chinook was first introduced in 1962 and is called a multi-mission helicopter. That means it's pretty good at doing virtually everything. It can carry people and it can be used to transport goods. This supercopter can even carry loads suspended from it on straps. This makes it useful in all sorts of places—from war zones and disaster areas to hard-to-reach oil rigs.

There are infrared searchlights on board. This is helpful for finding people at night.

The Chinook was designed for the US military, but it is now used by armed forces across the globe.

SUPER STATS

BOEING CH-47 CHINOOK
TOP SPEED: 160 knots (296 km/h)
POWERED BY: 2 x turboshaft engines
ENGINE POWER: 6,296 horsepower
CREW: 4
PASSENGERS: Up to 44
MAXIMUM ALTITUDE: 4,572 m
  (15,000 feet)
MADE IN: USA

MBB BO-105

Since the early days of the 20th century, watching planes do aerobatics, or stunts in the air, has been popular. But no one thought that doing a loop-the-loop in a helicopter was possible. That's until the MBB BO-105 came along! This agile aircraft is the top choice of helicopter for pilots who want to do aerobatics. This supercopter has responsive controls and a stable flying ability.

Unlike many helicopters, the BO-105 has what is called a rigid rotor system. This means the rotor blades are bolted straight to the rotor head at the top and not fixed to hinges. This is what makes this helicopter ideal for stunts.

Smoke canisters can be attached to the skids during displays.

In an aerobatic display, it's important to see what's around you. The BO-105's huge windows provide excellent visibility.

Originally, the MBB BO-105 wasn't designed for doing stunts. It was built as a multi-purpose helicopter and is used for a variety of very different jobs. Air forces strap missiles to the side of it and use it to destroy tanks. Construction companies use it to carry goods. Medical teams use it for emergencies. But in the hands of a skilled pilot, the BO-105 can really put on a display at an air show!

The rotor head (the part anchoring the rotor blades) is made from titanium, a light but very tough metal.

Aerobatics put a huge strain on the helicopter, so it has a specially strengthened frame to cope with all the difficult stunts.

The rotor blade edges are lined with aluminum to make them stronger.

The lightweight BO-105 is a real pleasure to fly.

SUPER STATS

MBB BO-105
TOP SPEED: 151 mph (243 km/h)
POWERED BY: 2 x turboshaft engines
ENGINE POWER: 860 horsepower
CREW: 1
PASSENGERS: 4
MAXIMUM ALTITUDE: 10,000 feet (3,050 m)
MADE IN: Germany

MEAN MACHINES

BOEING SIKORSKY RAH-66 COMANCHE

The best type of defense is not to be spotted in the first place. That's why the RAH-66 Comanche was such a fantastic supercopter. It was designed to be hard to see, hard to hear, and even hard to spot on radar. If you couldn't see it coming, it would have been very hard to shoot it down. This was great news for the pilots on board!

A bulletproof outer body offered excellent protection for the pilots.

Its strange shape made it difficult to spot on enemy radar machines.

Different sorts of missiles could be loaded to the Comanche. This made it as good at fighting as it was at hiding.

The Comanche was much quieter than normal helicopters thanks to the design of the main and tail rotors.

There's a reason why you won't have seen a Comanche helicopter and it's not just due to its clever technology. The Comanche never actually made it into production. Only a couple of prototypes were made, which makes this helicopter super-rare and super-stealthy. However, you can be sure that some of the technology they tried out first on the Comanche is being used on other top-secret stealth helicopters.

We don't know what the Comanche was made from—it's top secret! This material helped it hide from detection by radar.

The cockpit was sealed so the pilots couldn't be affected by chemical or biological weapons.

The Comanche was in development for around 22 years and is estimated to have cost about $4.5 billion!

SUPER STATS

BOEING SIKORSKY RAH-66 COMANCHE
TOP SPEED: 200 mph (324 km/h)
POWERED BY: 2 x turboshaft engines
ENGINE POWER: 2,864 horsepower
CREW: 2
PASSENGERS: 0
MAXIMUM ALTITUDE: Unknown
MADE IN: USA

KAMAN K-MAX UAS

Helicopters need at least one and sometimes two pilots to fly them. That's not true of the K-Max UAS, though. This remarkable machine doesn't need any pilots at all! It isn't as though the K-Max is a tiny remote-control toy. Actually, it's a full-sized helicopter designed for carrying heavy loads!

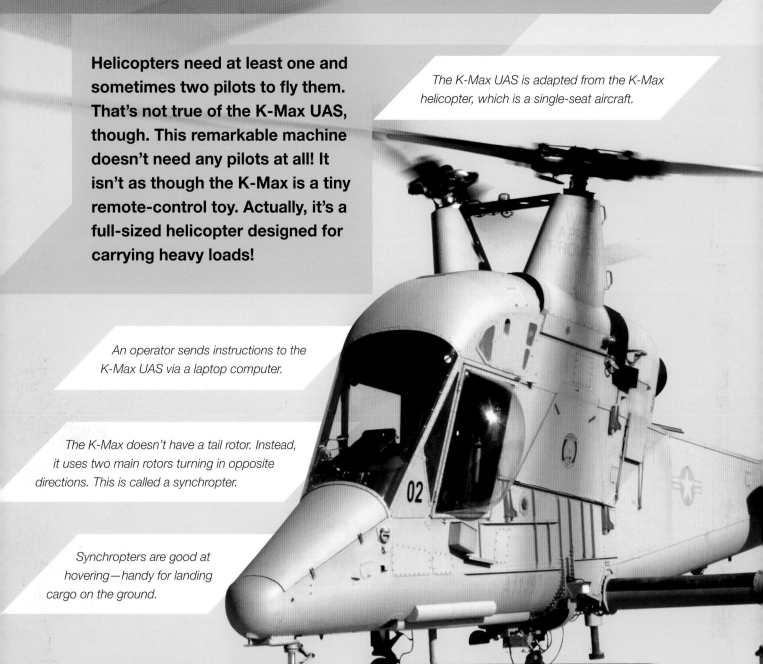

The K-Max UAS is adapted from the K-Max helicopter, which is a single-seat aircraft.

An operator sends instructions to the K-Max UAS via a laptop computer.

The K-Max doesn't have a tail rotor. Instead, it uses two main rotors turning in opposite directions. This is called a synchropter.

Synchropters are good at hovering—handy for landing cargo on the ground.

UAS stands for Unmanned Aerial System.

It goes without saying that battlefields are very dangerous places. Therefore, the best way to stay out of danger is not to be there in the first place. That's where the K-Max UAS comes in handy. The K-Max UAS is used to drop supplies in some of the most dangerous places in the world. It does this without having to risk the life of a pilot.

Cargo can be moved automatically along the helicopter's underside to keep it properly balanced.

There's a pilot's seat in the K-Max UAS, so the helicopter can still be flown in the traditional way.

Cargo is carried on four hooks below the helicopter.

SUPER STATS

KAMAN K-MAX UAS
TOP SPEED: 115 mph (185 km/h)
POWERED BY: 1 x gas turbine engines
ENGINE POWER: 1,800 horsepower
CREW: 0 (but there is room for 1)
PASSENGERS: 0
MAXIMUM ALTITUDE: 29,117 feet (8,875 m)
MADE IN: USA

GLOSSARY

aerobatics Stunts performed by an aircraft.

altitude The height of an object compared to sea or ground level.

aluminum A silvery-white metal used to make lightweight products.

cockpit The space in a plane, car, or boat where the pilot or driver sits.

infrared A color of light that cannot be seen by human eyes. Infrared radiation can be detected by cameras and search lights as heat.

knots A way of measuring the speed of aircraft and boats. 1 knot is equal to approximately 1.151 mph (1.852 km/h).

rotor A group of blades on a helicopter that rotate to lift the vehicle.

satellite An object that travels around a planet in a regular orbit.

surplus More than what is needed.

synchropter A helicopter with two main rotors that turn in different directions.

titanium A strong, silvery-gray chemical substance.

winch A machine with a rope or chain that is used for lifting or pulling objects.

FURTHER READING

Bodden Victoria. *Rescue Vehicles: Helicopters.* Creative Paperbacks, 2011.

Colson, Rob. *Helicopters* (Ultimate Machines). Powerkids Press, 2013

Dartford, Mark. *Helicopters.* Lerner, 2004.

Eason, Sarah. *How Does a Helicopter Work?* Gareth Stevens, 2011.

INDEX

Firefighting 14–15, 22–23

Helicopter speed record 4

Multi-mission helicopters 24–25

Police helicopters 16–17

Rescue vehicles 8–9, 12–13

Rolls–Royce 4–5, 6–7, 12–13

Skycranes 22–23

Stealth helicopters 28–29

Stunt helicopters 26–27

Vietnam War 15

VIP helicopters 20–21